Rain Forests

by Nancy Smiler Levinson

illustrated by Diane Dawson Hearn

NEW GUINEA

Count Raggi's bird

Holiday House / New York

For Merrill Joan Gerber,
who continues to inspire
N. S. L.

With thanks to Charlotte Lucas
And best wishes to Nancy Smiler Levinson
D. D. H.

Text copyright © 2008 by Nancy Smiler Levinson
Illustrations copyright © 2008 by Diane Dawson Hearn
All Rights Reserved
Printed and Bound in Malaysia
The art for this book was created with acrylic paint
on Strathmore paper.
www.holidayhouse.com
First Edition
Reading Level: 2.7
1 3 5 7 9 10 8 6 4 2

Library of Congress Cataloging-in-Publication Data
Levinson, Nancy Smiler.
Rain forests / by Nancy Smiler Levinson ;
illustrated by Diane Dawson Hearn.—1st ed.
p. cm.
ISBN 0-8234-1899-5
1. Rain forests—Juvenile literature.
2. Rain forest ecology—Juvenile literature.
I. Hearn, Diane Dawson, ill. II. Title.
Qh86.L48 2006
577.34—dc22
2004059785
ISBN-13: 978-0-8234-1899-2

baby
orangutan

king cobra

leaf insect

birdwing butterfly

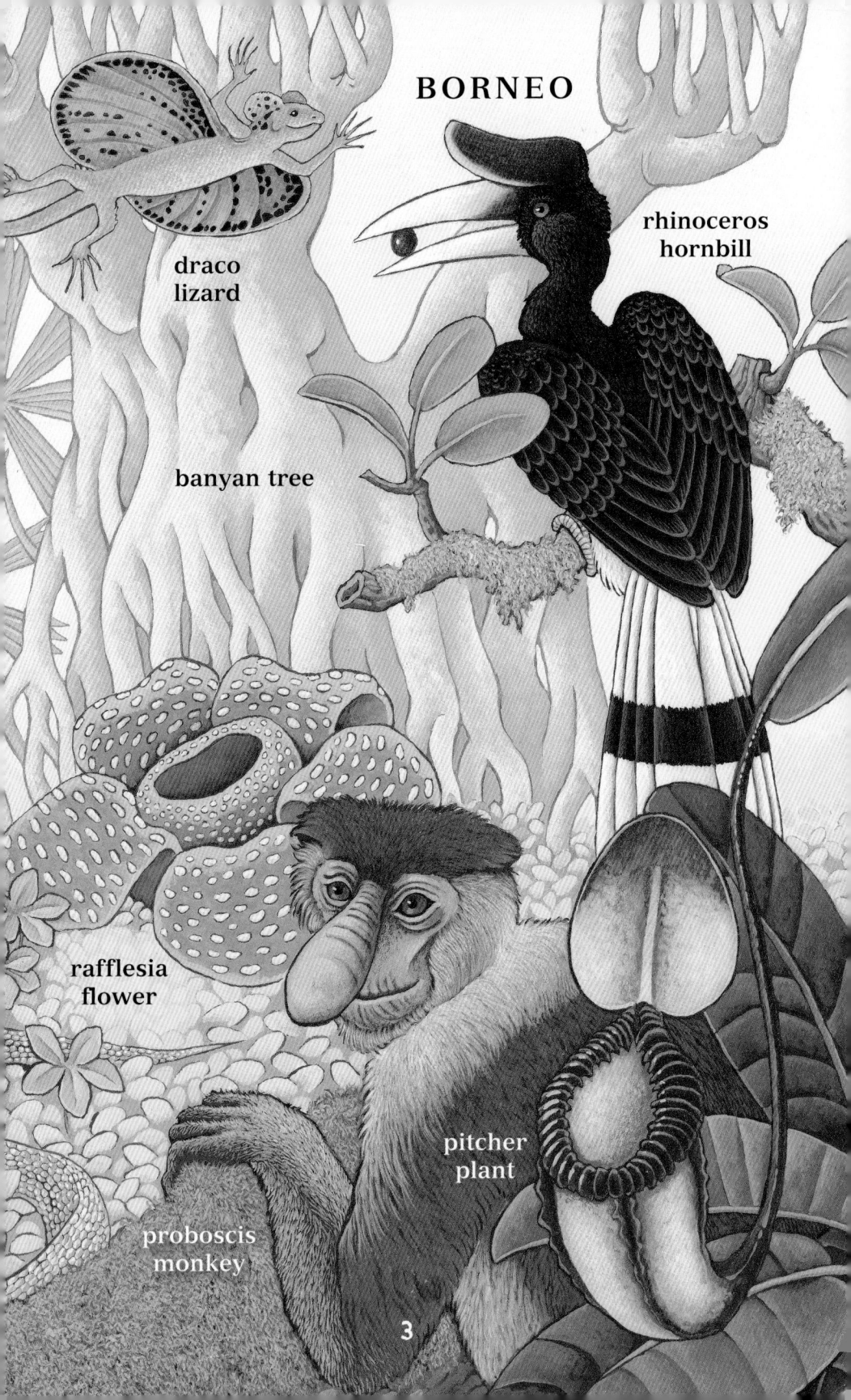

BORNEO

draco lizard

rhinoceros hornbill

banyan tree

rafflesia flower

pitcher plant

proboscis monkey

3

MADAGASCAR

comet moth

helmet bird

traveller's palm

red-ruffed lemur

4

A rain forest is a wet forest.
It is thick with many kinds of trees
and plants.
Many animals live in it.
Rain falls
most of the year.

silky
sifaka

giraffe-necked
weevil

Parson's
chameleon

Most rain forests grow in hot places
near the equator.
They are tropical rain forests.

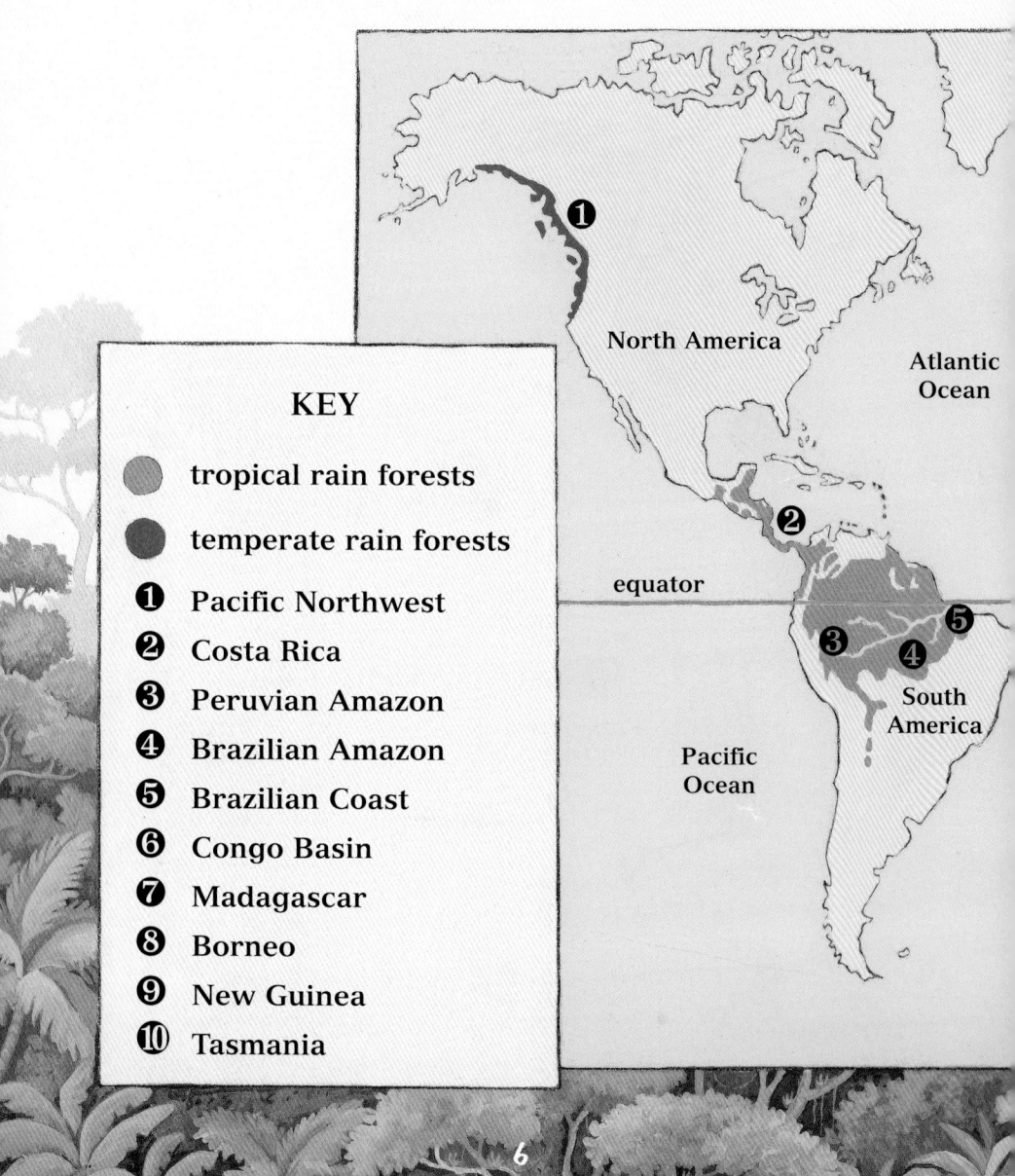

KEY

○ tropical rain forests

● temperate rain forests

❶ Pacific Northwest
❷ Costa Rica
❸ Peruvian Amazon
❹ Brazilian Amazon
❺ Brazilian Coast
❻ Congo Basin
❼ Madagascar
❽ Borneo
❾ New Guinea
❿ Tasmania

North America

Atlantic Ocean

equator

Pacific Ocean

South America

Some grow in cool places.

They are temperate rain forests.

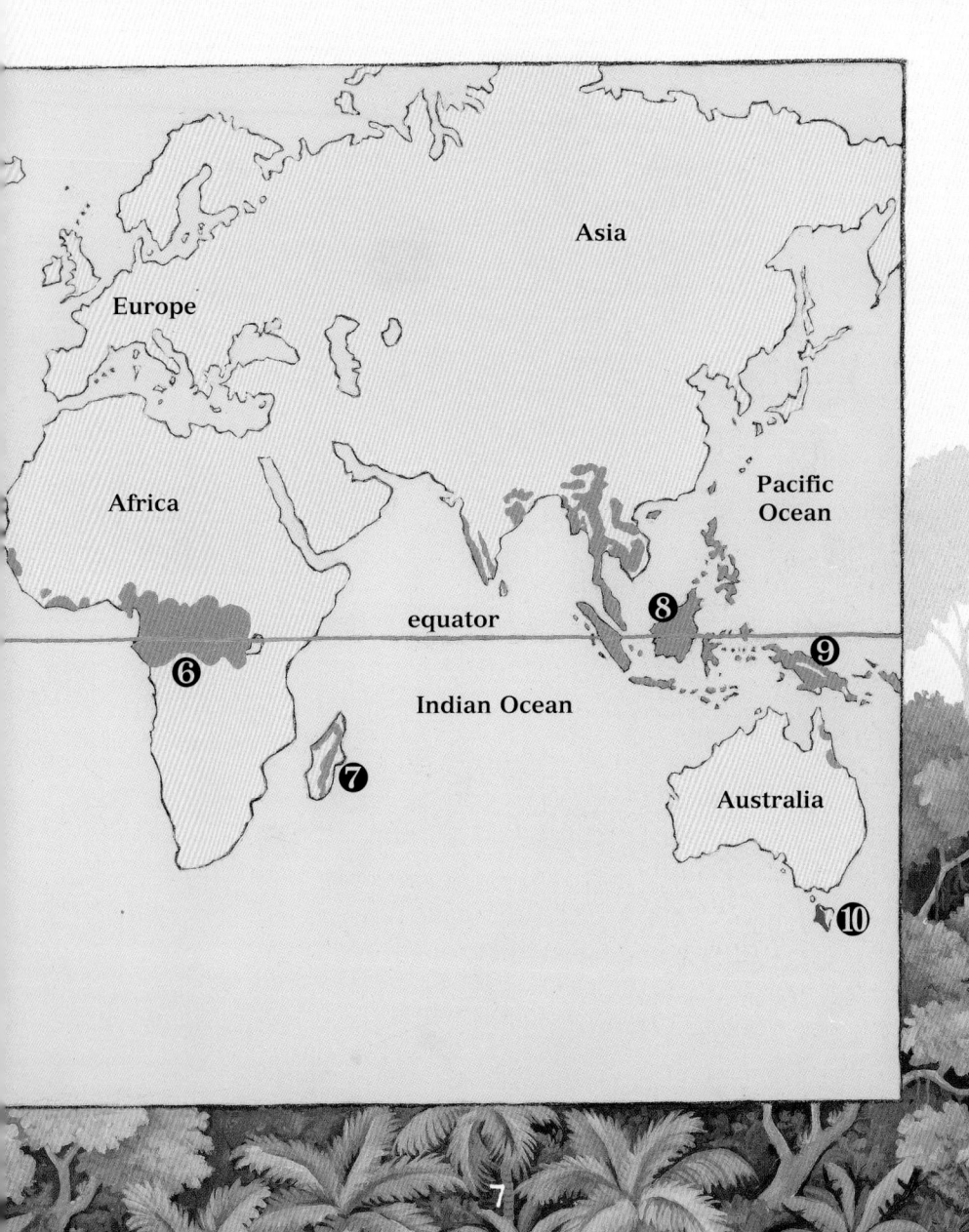

Asia

Europe

Africa

Pacific
Ocean

equator

❽

❾

❻

Indian Ocean

❼

Australia

❿

CONGO
BASIN

jade-headed
beetle

okapi

mahogany
tree

lowland
gorilla

bamboo

TROPICAL RAIN FORESTS

African
grey parrot

Tropical rain forests
are hot and wet.
How much rain falls every year?
Between 80 and 200 inches!
The temperatures stay
almost the same
every day.

mandrill

It is summer all the time.

pygmy
hippopotamus

white-throated toucan

palm fruit

ocelot

treehopper

mimosa butterfly

Tropical rain forests are jungles.
They are filled with trees, plants,
and vines.
Thousands of kinds
of animals live in them.

Peruvian
dung beetle

PERUVIAN AMAZON

hawk
moth
caterpillar

kapok tree
buttress

flag
bug

green
iguana

giant centipede

poison
dart frogs

One scientist found
forty-three kinds of insects
on one tree!
The world's largest tropical rain forest
is in the Amazon region
of South America.

firestick bug

Rain forests have four layers.

Each layer has its own life-forms.

The top layer is called *emergent*.

The emergent trees poke above

the rest of the forest into the sunlight.

Eagles and parrots live there.

red howler
monkeys

kapok
treetop

BRAZILIAN
AMAZON

harpy eagles

ipe tree

blue-headed parrots

13

The second layer is a closed *canopy*.
It is a living roof
that covers the forest below.
It is formed by treetops
that grow close together.

banana
tree

green-headed
tanager

gladiator
tree frog

spider
monkeys

scarlet
macaws

tayra

15

wasp

pygmy marmoset

yolk
butterfly

squirrel
monkey

monkey
ladder
vine

Monkeys eat berries and fruits.
Butterflies and hummingbirds
drink nectar from flowers.
Big stinging wasps
crawl across leaves.
This is the most lively layer of all.

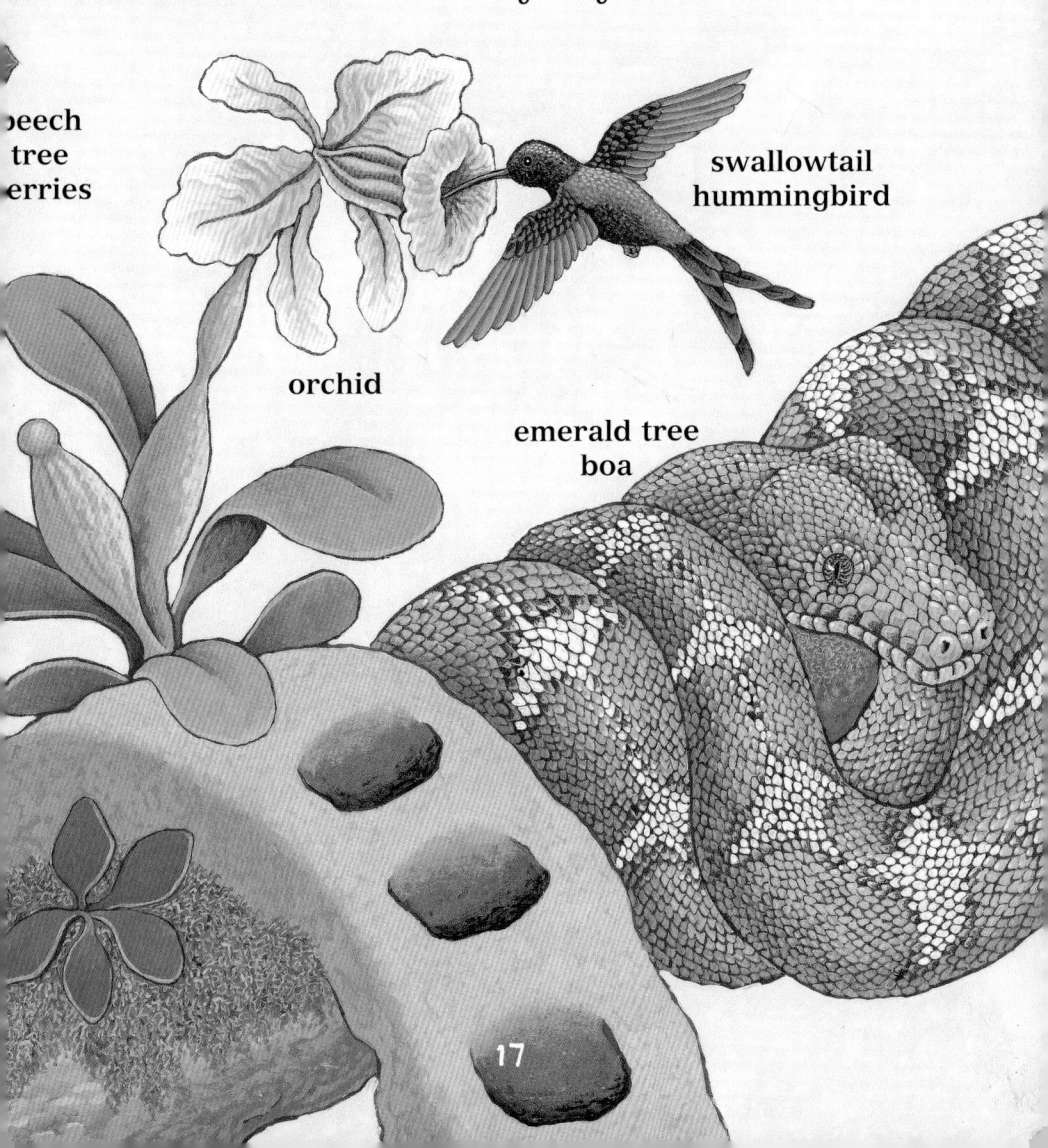

beech
tree
berries

swallowtail
hummingbird

orchid

emerald tree
boa

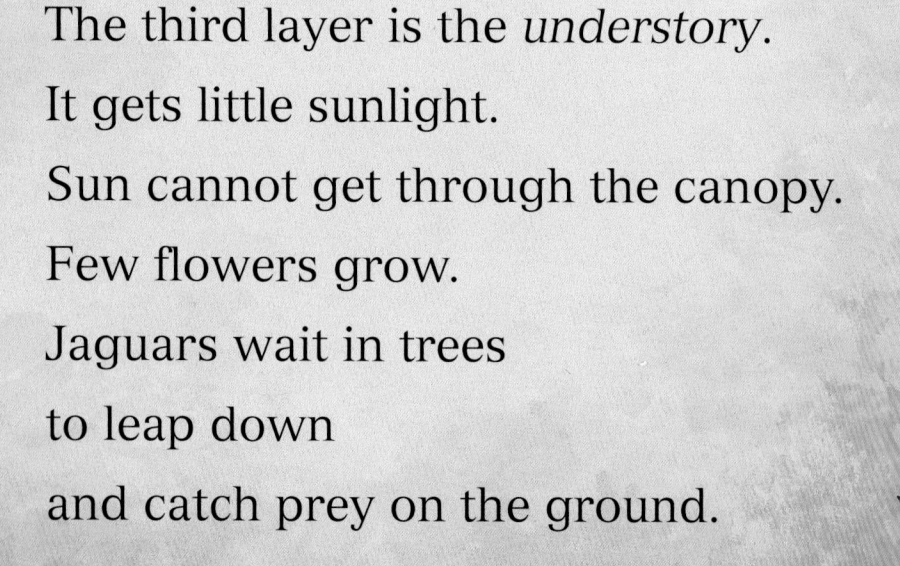

peperomia vine

jaguar

palm
fern

morpho
butterfly

staghorn
fern

The third layer is the *understory*.

It gets little sunlight.

Sun cannot get through the canopy.

Few flowers grow.

Jaguars wait in trees

to leap down

and catch prey on the ground.

cannonball
tree

coatimundi

mamey
tree

bare-faced
curassow

collared
puffbird

passion
flower
vine

vine
snake

coendou

moonflower

pigmy
owl

strangler
fig

anteater
(tamandua)

honeybear
(kinkajou)

20

Bats fly at night to feed.
Some catch three thousand insects
in one night's flight.

round-eared bats

sorcerer
moth

night monkey

vampire bat

The fourth layer is the *forest floor*.
It is dark and eerie.
It is filled with
plants, mosses, ferns, dead leaves,
and billions of ants.

ground
fern

capybara

caiman

apple snail

Victoria
amazonia
water lily

piranha

hoatzin
and baby

walking tree

green
anaconda

moss

leafcutter ants

Hercules beetle

23

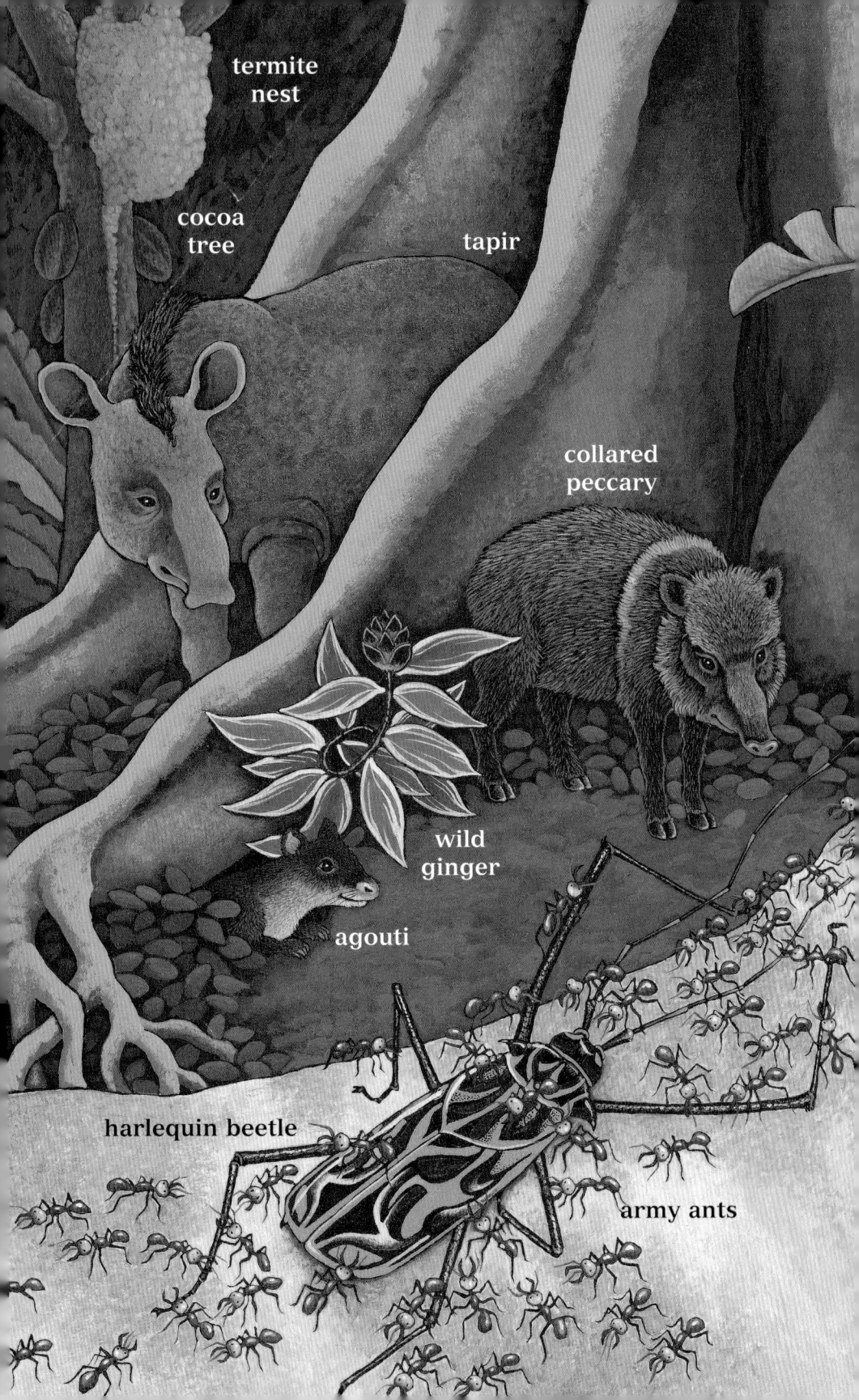

brocket
deer

heliconia

saddleback
caterpillar

pink-toed
tarantula

stink
beetle

Army ants march in swarms
and eat everything in their paths.
Termites live in colonies and eat wood.
Deer and wild pigs are hard to see,
but insects can be seen everywhere!

three-toed
sloth

Many animals live in the trees
most of their lives.
Some tree frogs never touch the ground.
They have sticky toe pads
to help them climb slippery leaves.
Sloths hang upside down all the time—
even when they eat and sleep.

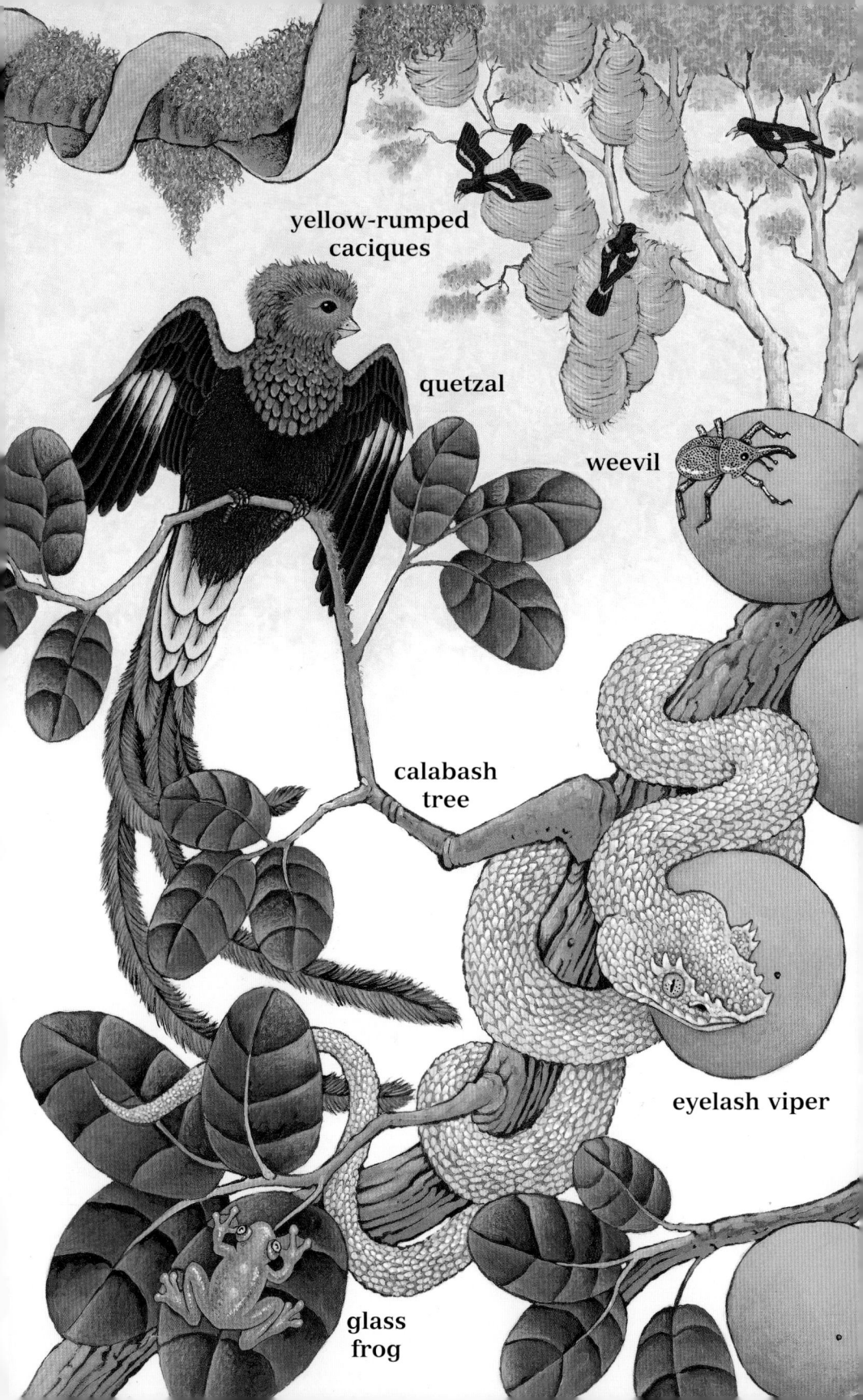

yellow-rumped
caciques

quetzal

weevil

calabash
tree

eyelash viper

glass
frog

Most plants need roots in soil
to get water and food.
Air plants do not.
They grow on tree trunks and
get water and food from the air.
They are called *epiphytes*.
Orchids and bromeliads
are epiphytes.

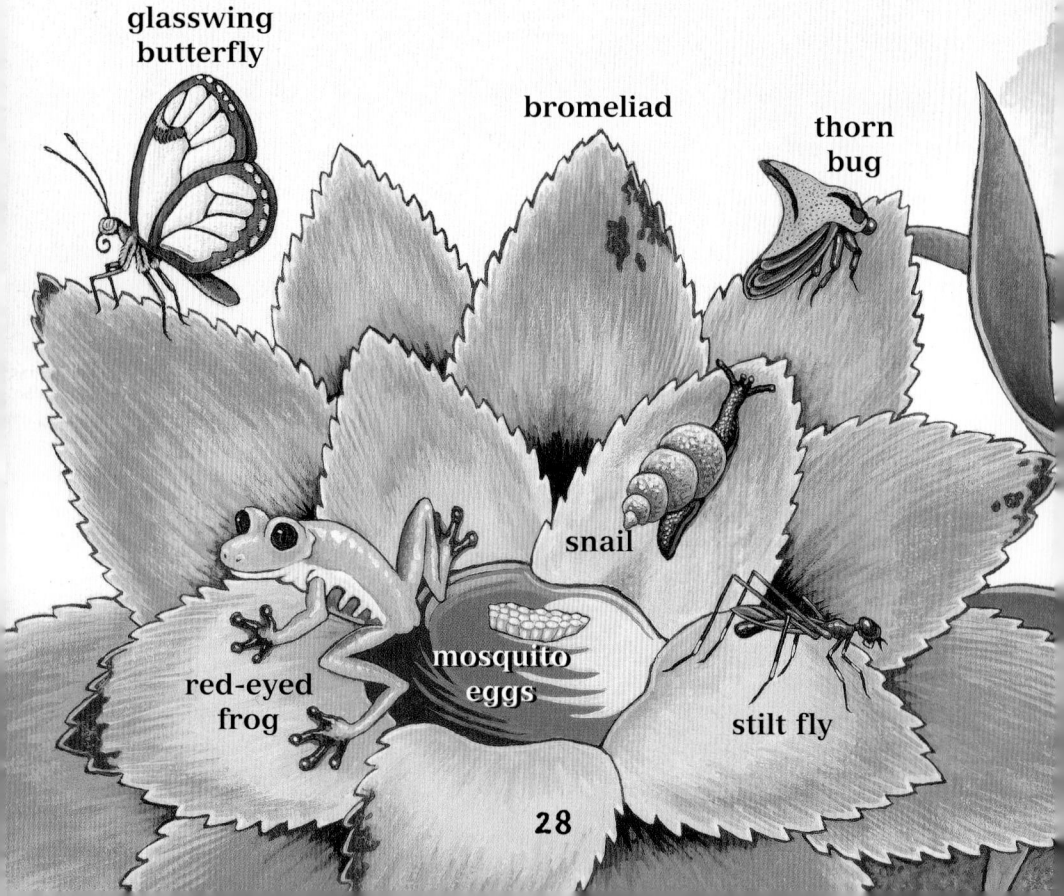

glasswing
butterfly

bromeliad

thorn
bug

snail

red-eyed
frog

mosquito
eggs

stilt fly

COSTA RICA

orchid

fiery-throated
hummingbird

bromeliad

scarab
beetle

orchid

bromeliad

capuchin
monkey

northern
spotted
owl

Sitka
spruce

bald eagle

licorice
fern

mule
deer

PACIFIC
NORTHWEST

cougar

black bear cub

TEMPERATE RAIN FORESTS

Most temperate rain forests grow

in the Pacific Northwest

of North America.

How much rain falls every year?

About 100 inches!

The seasons do change.

Fog and mist from the Pacific Ocean

bring warm summers and cool winters.

Temperate rain forests have layers, too.

But they do not look

like tropical rain forests.

Sun rays shine down to the forest floor.

Some trees are giant old-growth trees.

A Sitka spruce may be a thousand years old!

Tongass National Forest in Alaska
is the largest temperate rain forest
in the United States.
Rain forests grow along
the western side
of the Olympic Peninsula
in Washington State, too.
Most animals, such as squirrels, elks,
and porcupines,
live on the forest floor.
The Olympic forest is alive
with plants, too.

bobcat

devil's club

Indian pipe

Borneo

Congo
basin

Pacific Northwest

PEOPLE

People have lived in rain forests
for thousands of years.
They have hunted, fished, and farmed.
They have learned how to use plants
for medicines.

Amazon

Today more and more people
are coming to the rain forests.
They are clearing land
to farm and ranch.
They are cutting down trees
for lumber and paper.
They are hurting the rain forests.

People around the world
are working to find ways
to help protect the rain forests
of our earth.

Tropical Rain Forests

They grow in hot places near the equator.

They are found mostly in Central and South America, Central Africa, Southeast Asia, and northern Australia.

They do not have a dry season.

The temperatures are always warm.

The average rainfall is 80 to 100 inches a year.

The Amazon region in South America is the largest rain forest.

Most animals live in the canopy layer.

Temperate Rain Forests

They grow in cool places.

They are found mostly
in the Pacific Northwest of North America
and in Tasmania in southern Australia.

They have different seasons—
warm, foggy summers and cool winters.

Temperatures range from 80°F to freezing.

The average rainfall is 100 inches a year.

Tongass National Park in Alaska is the largest
temperate rain forest.

Most animals live on the forest floor.

ACKNOWLEDGMENTS

Many thanks to Regina Griffin, a special, astute editor of easy readers, and Charles F. Bennett, PhD, Professor Emeritus, Department of Geography, University of California, Los Angeles, for his assistance in the preparation of this book. And special thanks to the illustrator, Diane Dawson Hearn.   N. S. L

The publisher would like to thank Louis N. Sorkin of the American Museum of Natural History and educational consultant Melissa Wimer for their help.

BRAZILIAN COASTAL FOREST

golden
lion
tamarin